HAIL, THE INVISIBLE WATCHMAN

HAIL, THE INVISIBLE WATCHMAN

ALEXANDRA OLIVER

BIBLIOASIS
Windsor, Ontario

FIRST EDITION

Library and Archives Canada Cataloguing in Publication

Title: Hail, the invisible watchman / Alexandra Oliver.
Names: Oliver, Alexandra, 1970- author.
Description: Poems.
Identifiers: Canadiana (print) 20210317035 | Canadiana (ebook) 20210317051 | ISBN 9781771964715
 (softcover) | ISBN 9781771964722 (ebook)
Classification: LCC PS8629.L54 H35 2022 | DDC C811/.6—DC23

Edited by Jason Guriel
Copyedited by John Sweet
Text and cover designed by Vanessa Stauffer
Cover photograph by Stephen Duffy

Published with the generous assistance of the Canada Council for the Arts, which last year invested $153 million to bring the arts to Canadians throughout the country, and the financial support of the Government of Canada. Biblioasis also acknowledges the support of the Ontario Arts Council (OAC), an agency of the Government of Ontario, which last year funded 1,709 individual artists and 1,078 organizations in 204 communities across Ontario, for a total of $52.1 million, and the contribution of the Government of Ontario through the Ontario Book Publishing Tax Credit and Ontario Creates.

PRINTED AND BOUND IN CANADA

For Kim Bridgford
1959–2020

CONTENTS

HAIL, THE INVISIBLE WATCHMAN

THE HAUNTING OF SHERBET LAKE

The way this knowledge gathered in me was the strangest thing in the world—the strangest, that is, except the very much stranger in which it quickly merged itself. I had sat down with a piece of work—for I was something or other that could sit— on the old stone bench which overlooked the pond; and in this position I began to take in with certitude, and yet without direct vision, the presence, at a distance, of a third person.
HENRY JAMES, THE TURN OF THE SCREW

YOUNG POLITICIAN AT A ROTARY CLUB TEA

There's that woman running for the council,
eating cake. Her selfie arm is spangled,
tan and toned and perfect as a pencil.
Imagine how the sallow mayor tingled
guiltily, the moment that he met her.
She has a plan to make the city better;
she's born and bred in Sherbet Lake. She knows
how older noses love an English Rose.
She understands the darkness to the letter.

Her website is explosively sincere
with photos from the cookouts and parades:
her python grip around the engineer
who made it through the marathon, the spades
in suffocating soil, the Wizard's Ball
(a benefit for the hospital's new hall)
where, stiff in silk, gripping a flute of cava,
she grins. The posted comments flow like lava;
she lies awake at night. She reads them all.

The matrons of the town were apprehensive;
the masters thought her age might make her bold
but, luckily, her views were unexpansive
and, happily, she fit the tribal mould:
(dimpled triplets, dogs, a decent guy).
She's never once been compromised or high
but peppers her talk with *heritage* and *tradition*,
flutters the nation's flag at the right occasion
and swears that Sherbet Lake is where she'll die.

When I was thirty-one, I never thought
I'd want to wade into a chittering crowd
and butter up the biddies, remain untaught
by what was free and dangerous and loud,
but here you are, nodding over your cake
and longing for the spear of Sherbet Lake.
That Etch A Sketch of wealth and same and sorrow:
perhaps you'll take it in your hands tomorrow,
admire their work.
                    Or shake and shake and shake.

PIEROGIS

That was the one thing that we couldn't have.
Our dad avoided Slavic peasant fare,
having donned a Britishness so flawless
it cloaked the Jewish refugee within,
rustling brusquely in tweed and silk pyjamas.
He had no time for diasporic dramas;
roast at the Savoy, the perfect gin,
a summer pudding, lucent as a cutlass,
all turned his crank. Pierogis equalled fear,
fear of folklore, dybbuks, doors, lost love—

but I had a latchkey friend when I was eight
(with glamorous parents whom I'd never seen);
tall, red-headed, cheery as a lark,
she had me over, made me you-know-whats,
using a real microwave (the danger!).
In a kitchen free from adult eyes and anger
(and grandmothers, wilted tea towels, spitting pots),
we scarfed the carbs and, glutted with youth and dark,
locked eyes and licked the heavy flatware clean
as ABBA crooned and the moon replaced the daylight

and I got the grand tour, too (when we were done):
kilometres of shag, a silent pool,
a reel-to-reel, a disco floor, a den.
The master bedroom was a work of art:
raised on a dais like an Aztec shrine,
the bed, a bloated satin Valentine,

was flanked by mags with names like *Spank* and *Squirt*
and buzzing toys. I swirled my tongue again
for hidden remainders, thrilled to be bad at all
but wearing the pious shock of a Polish nun.

Years later, down at our big-box store,
the Favourite is handed out in cups
on Sample Day. The woman in the net,
a brittle local, has no village in her,
but rather breathes the air of Old Stock smug
(the twitching drapes, the *Tremble, Snowflake!* mug).
She boils the dumplings, flops them into a strainer
(wiping her brow in the skillet's droning heat),
sighs and shakes, picks up the cleaver, chops,
plucks and places, then surveys the floor.

Why do they say *no*? It's always hidden,
the reason why we can't have what delights us.
A slender woman approaches the display,
surprised and smiling. A toddler clutches her dress.
She thinks, *ah, Manti!* (maybe of her mother),
and reaches for a cup. Faced with the other,
in a prim charade of suburban politesse,
the sample lady clucks, sweeps up the tray.
They're not for you. Stunned by the sightless,
the stranger walks towards me, away from the forbidden.

SEVENTEEN

Seventeen circle the rim of the gym,
in orbit around the instructor who yells
and yells and yells. They listen to him.
(The fathers, in hopefulness, peer from the halls.)

Seventeen scissor their legs on the mats,
slashing the air, like quick little knives.
They are told to develop their glutes and their lats.
(The fathers remember their whey-coloured wives.)

Seventeen shoulder their bags to the courts—
their elders assure them it's not about winning—
but wince, as the possible pecks at their hearts.
(The fathers are fat and their forelocks are thinning.)

Seventeen play to the darkening hours,
then peel off in columns, exhausted and little.
They go to the washrooms and tremble in mirrors.
(The fathers bare teeth, lemon-tinted and brittle.)

Seventeen eight-year-old creatures are moving;
they climb into vans. As if speaking to God,
they venture, *I think that I'm really improving.*
The fathers hit gas and set fire to the road.

BRYCE MCMILLAN, 38, FUTURES TRADER, STUCK AT THE MEN'S RETREAT

Putting aside the man-child making
spent span of wasted
energy and great sacks of money,
now I've entered a world of waking;
now my soul's tasted
the bliss of a realm flowing with honey.

So I must cash in my chips and lose
manners of the wildebeest
and that thing for Tesla and Celine.
Shall I admit I miss the lakes of booze
and find no fine feast
in the hot volley of tofu and bean,

the muddled cuddle yoga in the Great Tent?
I often wonder
what happened to my iPhone and my silk socks;
with no one here to listen to me vent,
I may go under,
pummel the camp bicycle with rocks.

Yearning to fly past the warm, embracing
tales of my own birth,
brought on by the chants, the calm nods of my brother,
now I fear, with my bloodstream racing,
that our Mother Earth
is a heartless bitch, bro. I want my real mother.

SONG OF THE DOYENNE

The Doyenne was top of the heap in this town.
Her parents were wealthy as Croesus,
and the pearl of the future was all hers to own
while everyone else went to pieces.
Her husband got taller, her children more clever;
the house on the block kept expanding forever.
In a place where the liars laid low,
the Doyenne desired to grow.

She sidled her way to the sides of the women
who seemed to be new and untested.
Her smile had the uniform crispness of linen
so none of them ever protested.
They came to her home and they sipped on her wine;
they felt themselves wilt in the heat and the shine
until, when the spell was undone,
the Doyenne devoured the sun.

The ones that she chose were awash in their fears;
their firmaments roiled with trouble.
Their problems with money had aged them by years
and half of their kin were unstable.
And when they decided they'd someone to trust,
they told the Doyenne, who dissolved in disgust
and dropped them and left with no traces,
well shot of their middle-drawer faces.

The Doyenne is top of the heap in this town,
a legend, if shorter and squatter.
Embarrassments found her, a freight all her own,
but that is a personal matter.
She threw in her lot with the silvery others—
the affluent, arrogant, terrified mothers.
To thank her, I'll give my mind's eye:
I've made sure the Doyenne won't die.

SCHOOLTEACHER REPORT I (2016)

I've seen that type of child before, she said,
scrabbling inside her desk to find a pen,
they question what you say because they *can,*
go on and on about something they read.
They like to sit together, calm and sneering,
refusing to match their manners to your size,
swallow your words with wide, unblinking eyes,
preen as a flock, give their pride an airing.
They stare you down, wide-smiling, pencil poised,
clean-collared and callow. Raising their wax-smooth hands
to tell you the height, the date, the rule of thumb.
But they know I have a way to handle boys,
the arsenic that simmers in their glands.
They know I know what they will all become.

SCHOOLTEACHER REPORT II (1975 / 2013)

Divorced and derailing, we knew she was trouble—
you could tell where she was by her curses,
red-headed, turtlenecked, clinking with bangle,
smacking her stick on the verb and the angle.
She labelled the slower ones *soulless*
and feathered her nest with our smallness.
She didn't like chatter or sneaker skid either
and once threw a packet of gum at my brother.

Beaten and paling, as frail as a bubble—
we saw her, a week before Christmas,
out with her carer at Bushell and Myrtle.
She sounded delighted. We tried to be gentle
and show the old duck she was blameless
but levelled our weapons with murderous wholeness.
My teacher disaster, take notice and wither:
what you have sown you must gather.

THE ANNOUNCER

Our supers once had the brass to boss a helper
into tears, the aptitude for fiction,
the knack of rattling a boardroom sabre
and waving a bad soufflé back to the kitchen.

But Francis sank their money in a Ponzi.
They lost the Jag, the home with twenty rooms,
and went from being Bay Street's Sid and Nancy
to cursing softly from behind their brooms.

Charred and muted by the ream of changes,
of poking in our washers with a wrench,
of reinstalling cupboards on their hinges,
and scrubbing darker matter off the bench,

Lou fell silent.
                    That was until The Firm
installed the PA speakers in each suite,
democratizing each false fire alarm
that poured befuddled tenants into the street.

She liked to give the drill's placating coda
in which she chirped the worst of it was over
and felt the old omniscient persona
take hold, the heft of bringing doom or closure,

and soon moved on to squeezing in the latest
(parking fees, the closure of the gym)

then what was on her mind—the hidden greatness
of her chiropractor. The quiet scam

of marriage and the treachery of churches,
the asps of hope that slither through our lives.
She intercommed her wild, despairing purchase
on truth. But, here, no one like that survives.

They let Lou go for being loud and odd
but she moved on, knowing the creed by heart:
It is the voice cast large that copies God.
It is the voice cast large that forges art.

TALKING TO A CHILD ABOUT SEPTICEMIA, 2010
For James Merrill

All interest in disease and death is only
another expression of interest in life.
THOMAS MANN

Is he strong? Listen, bud!
He's got radioactive blood.
PAUL FRANCIS WEBSTER AND ROBERT "BOB" HARRIS,
   "SPIDER-MAN" THEME SONG

One's blood is like the tide:
scattered with life that floats,
red music with assorted notes.
This is the song where cells and pride collide.

Some say it overturns,
and some say no,
this kind of illness has no strong
arm, though one can feel how, feel how it burns.

It shares a course with anger and with shame,
lighting the veins like tracks on a map,
radioactive, bright with wild choler and flame.

But also (like the worst we know)
joy-rivers thunder—yes, inside:
blood on fire. What? Oh.

What is its source?
Like whom, you say? Like Spider-Man. Of course.

HOLLYWOOD. NORTH.

Enter the actors. They're rich in credential.
Their agency pages exhibit their charm:
They've triumphed in golf on an After-School Special
and shielded the crew of a shuttle from harm.
They've featured as coppers and strippers and spies,
a walk-on appearance as lawyer or doctor,
a dangerous alien in the disguise
of a different alien driving a tractor
through sad fields of lettuce on somebody's farm.

Enter the actors. The locals, the specials.
The coastal celebrities, gusseted, glossed.
They've worked in the wilderness, hiding their bushels
under their lights, or wait (am I lost?),
the other way round. They've slaved for their dinners;
they've seated the lofty at sushi emporia,
wheeled on their sunniest teeth-flashing manners
while peddling fake leather pants at Aritzia,
striving for starlight, whatever the cost.

Enter the actors. They come to the party
in plummeting garments and collars of feathers
and wonder if thirty still means that they're pretty
and should they keep trying if nobody bothers.
They've never known seagulls or longing for Moscow
or poked at a manuscript eaten by flames,
or scrubbed off the blood from their fingers in sorrow,
but look into our faces repeating their names:
their own, their own, not the others', the others'.

BACON

The only thing is, I'm wearing a micro-skirt and my bacon is
stuck to the chair.
<small>TWITTER POST BY A 17-YEAR-OLD USER (GERMANY),
     MAY 2017. LIKES: 102.</small>

I read about the bacon and the chair
and find your coyness smartly underhand;
I think we might agree there's something there.

You're just a blur of milk and sable hair;
I picture you in spandex on the sand
(I read about the bacon and the chair).

Perhaps you'll have an afternoon to spare;
you need an older man's proficient hand
to put you in your place and keep you there.

I'm married, yes. But she's agreed to share
(conventional monogamy be damned!).
I read about the bacon and the chair.

They say I'm still a catch (some wear and tear,
but being seasoned keeps you in demand).
There's something in attainment, isn't there?

The changes in me drive me to despair;
but girls, like grass and stars, may understand.
I read about the bacon and the chair;
how miserable I am I found it there.

THE LAST STRAW OF THE LAST DUCHESS

I'm his last duchess, hanging on the wall,
though as to why, I know sweet bugger all.
I didn't mind the dress they put me in.
Fra Pandolf said he had to see more skin
but that's an artist for you. So one day,
I turn fourteen and my old man says, hey,
there's someone that we'd like to bring around
for dinner. And he's nothing too profound,
a skinny raisin who looks like he could use
a little sun. So how can I refuse?
I've always been considered pretty game,
and, as for that nine-hundred-years-old name,
so what? Well, things get rolling just as you
might think they would. I have to take a few
catch-up classes: catechism, Greek,
and needlepoint. It gets a little bleak:
I mix the popes and make a royal mess
of tapestries. It's anybody's guess
how someone could survive a house of bores
who clack and thump across the marble floors.
I never see Alfonso; he's off starting
fortress restoration groups and carting
people round the place to see the spoils.
I'm not that much for noblemen in oils,
or stony Roman torsos, mute and stern.
There's always some new bloodiment, an urn,
a moor, a suit of armour. Lately Claus,
some Austrian, just dragged into the house

a sea horse (cast in bronze), who's being tamed
by some nude Neptune. (Gross! I'm so ashamed!)
You're better off just doing your own thing.
I stroll the garden path in early spring
alone or with the dogs, and watch the sun
arc past the trees until its course is done.
I see it sink, I get eaten by that gold.
An office memo says I'm just too bold
with other men, but really, that's my style,
so what's the problem with a passing smile?
I'm just a *people person,* that's my point.
I'm sorry if his nose is out of joint
but, in this life, you have to make the best
of what you've got. Is this some kind of test
to see if he's collected *me?* Let's say
he never made it clear in any way;
I try to turn him on to all the nice
things *I* like: cherries, flowers, sun. (No dice.)
I pass him on the mule, he shrugs his bulk
and slips off, in a black, unstooping sulk.
The house fills up with musty hunks of art
until he cracks. (*The party's over, tart.*)
And now I have to listen to that squeak,
the curtain pulled aside six times a week,
and give it all to him, these quiet stares
in moments linking art and state affairs.
If I weren't here and painted like the dead,
I'd hurl that fucking sea horse at his head.

THE LIPSTICK EFFECT

You know you need a new one when you're bored
or overcome or underwhelmed or sad,
when you can feel the jangles of your age;
when vapours fill the valleys of your mind
(the news, your kids, the heft of your behind)—
or change arrives, the turning of a page:
you lose a job, move house, cremate your dad,
then add another colour to the hoard

amassed in your boudoir. Their names alone
inspire revolution at some level,
assuring you there's Fire Down Below
a Pirate, Lustering lust, a latent Vamp,
a Dolce Vita waiting where you camp,
and, on the prairie, Cherries in the Snow.
Beneath the paint, you're neither sleek nor evil.
It's just the tubes, the hollow names, you own.

HOW TO STOP

The hefty boots are padded, stitched in pink,
as if to comfort you you're still a lady
in them, though you're armoured like a tank
at elbow, knee, and wrist, your helmet ready—

shuffling through the parking lot at nightfall
while, upstairs, locals sit, caressing glasses
(far away from asphalt and its peril)
in unwheeled pumps and unprotective dresses.

While they chat, bend forward to the bowl
of Terra chips, pour rum into their pop,
can they hear the skid, the crash, the howl,
the woman in the lot who cannot stop?

Later, can they see you, all fatigue,
trawling YouTube for the latest tips
on slowing down (*Kick out! Drag your leg!
Squat! Pigeon toes! Keep shoulders over hips!*)?

Answer: no. You wriggle into bed
at fifty-one, dream you're on the path,
a bolt of lightning, knowing what you should:
the only thing that slows you down is death.

THE CREATURES

When we were young, our friendships just appeared
out of the air, the sea, an open door,
uncalled as if by magic. They were ours,
uncurated by our folks' desires.
We stumbled onto our friends by playground benches
or lumped in basements at our parents' parties.
When older and escaped, we found them waiting:
they served us in a bar then reappeared
as girlfriend to a guy in someone's band.
We ended up one night in an ivied house:
creaseless, single, shrieking at the film,
swilling Jägermeister from the bottle
as Deborah Kerr, the gasping governess,
panted out her Freudian distress.

When we get older, something starts to happen:
We drift apart from the accidents we cherished
and move away to gentle, twittering streets
with partners or with children or alone.
We sink into the things we want or own,
dishes, gardens, vehicles, vacations.
We land appalling jobs and start performing,
spiriting money out of screens and paper
to buy ourselves the clothes we won't be seen in.
We paint our mouths and saunter through the dusk,
knowing well that no one will ask the time
or tell us that our hair has grown a little
or meet us at the taco place for wine
to reassure us that we turned out fine.

So what do we do? We *make* the friends instead:
plunge our hands into the placid earth,
decide that we're still fun enough to fashion
someone worthy of our full attention.
We spend the hours, whistling and trying
to pat our love into the silent limbs,
shaping the ears that hear us when we prattle,
cocking the brows to make them read as funny.
We make a golem out of sad park mud,
the doorstop dust, the feathers on the wind,
pinioning companions in our longing,
giving them names and shortening our own
when leaving messages *(It's Allie! Call me!)*,
waiting for closeness to set, to blossom slowly.

But none of these mud-ones slogged through the fire fields
of puberty or held us when we cried
the night we were dumped by some oily drummer
or law school drone or Kitsilano stoner.
They never pointed out our bosses were creepy
and that it might be better just to quit
and hit the open road. They never flung
their pebbles at our shutters, phoned to ask
if they could write love letters at our desks,
or show up saying, If we leave right now,
the two of us could make it to Seattle
in three hours flat, watch the vista lighten,
see the sun rise over the Ballard boats
while shivering in one another's coats.

No, what you get is the flat-eyed school-gate falcon,
studded bright with the nails of a moneyed marriage.

You get the couple who come over to eat,
put down their forks in undefined offence
at something that you said in another life,
then leave and never contact you again.
You get the guy who sees you as a prize,
a gunner in some heartless female army,
and, drunk, you ask the office to your place
one shimmering night, after the Christmas party,
then stand at the balcony waiting as no one arrives,
as the mud below rattles its diamond tail
and hisses indifferently, as if to say
Save yourself. Save it all.
                    Slowly back away.

THE VAMPIRE LOVERS

Occasionally the movies go mad. They have terrifying
visions; they erupt in visions that show the true face of society.
Fortunately, however, they are healthy at the core. Their
schizophrenic outbursts last only a few moments, then the
curtain is lowered again and everything returns to normal.
SIEGFRIED KRACAUER, "THE LITTLE SALESGIRLS GO
    TO THE MOVIES" (1927)

Hail, the invisible watchman,
silent and pale as a swan,
older than anything human,
spectral and silver and silken,
curled in the wakening dawn.
Why were the daughters so fearless?
Why did they go to the gate
and why did they dare to be careless—
didn't they know they were bait
for him, the invisible watchman?

Hail, the invisible watchman.
On screen he would gamely appear,
preening and lounging and luring.
Everything else became boring;
nothing was needed or near.
Daily they followed his actions,
cursed his invisible wife,
muffled their other attractions,
swore they were branded for life
by him, the invisible watchman.

Hail, the invisible watchman;
the parents are panicked and lost.
The daughters aren't eating or dancing.
In school, they are hardly advancing;
their fingers are frozen with frost.
Their elders declare he will vanish,
and tell them that he is not real
but nothing will lessen the anguish
and nothing will sweeten the deal
beyond the invisible watchman.

Hail, the invisible watchman:
angular, mottled, and keen,
older than anything human.
See: he is plotting your ruin—
now, when you're done with routine,
done with the soup and the sweeping,
when you are lying in bed,
next to a ghost who is sleeping,
he will be with you instead,
he, the invisible watchman.

PROTECTIVE

"Love must be put into action!"
screamed the old hermit.
ELIZABETH BISHOP, "CHEMIN DE FER"

They say that Arthur Jensen is insane.
He cycles dawn to dusk and doesn't eat
(which would explain the John the Baptist frame).
At sixty-five, his torment is complete:
torment meaning toplessness. Leather shorts,
the clinking of a cock ring at his throat,
his diva role in neighbourly reports:
how he lures the unsuspecting widows out
or spends the evenings barking like a dog
or rolls around in pentacles and feces
or dresses like a woman. He's been pinned
as *deviant* and *lunatic* and *fag,*
and every time he stops to tie his laces,
some say he sends a scent downwind.

I'll take our Arthur Jensen any day;
he doesn't haunt the laundry room with sneers
or frolic in the same suburban lie,
blasting his Coldplay after seven beers.
He doesn't cluck through polyester lace
nor make the case for Jesus in the lobby,
nor does he hum, like a dumb electric fence,
about the colour of the cashier's baby.
He's none of those cruel, daisy-fresh things
that sickened up the street before the lockdown

but rather he'll put love back into action,
sparkling uncle unhoused, hot pants and rings,
and this is where we show our faces at sundown
and supplicate for Arthur J.'s protection.

MRS BERYL ARMSTRONG, 86, BEATS CLOSING TIME AT LONGO'S

Today I have salami and a pear.
The line ahead creeps on. A buzzer rings;
an office girl is counting out her things
(what office needs a girl with purple hair?).
If I could stand upright, I'd see the sun
pouring over Fairview, gilding air
and awning. But I don't suppose I can.

I used to be a cracker, way back when,
but left a trail in Cereals last week.
They said, *It's all right, love,* and cleaned the muck.
I'll never hand my stockings to a man
or make a younger rival fall apart.
Outside, a boy takes out a violin,
but all I hear is someone digging dirt.

TRIPTYCH: AMERICAN WIVES

1630

This is the house on the rock that we founded:
that's what we say every time that you ask.
Here is your mother, here is your father.
The corn is destroyed and the clouds are wild
but this is why you've become our child,
you'll stay alive if we stay together.
Steady your gun as the others go past.
Don't fall asleep. They have you surrounded.

1865

This is the house with the beeches and pond.
That's where you sit with your bustle and jet,
here in the parlour, ignoring your ardour,
stitching his name on the little white gown;
another lost child is a treasure you own—
a bud on the orchid, a jar in the larder.
No one has written your elegy yet,
howled out your name in the hope you'll respond.

1956

This is the house with the big picture window,
that's what you wanted for hundreds of years:
a washing machine and a waist like a keyhole,
the coming of night and the crowing of stars
and the satellites up there that aren't even ours
as you wait at the centre, as dumb as a maypole,
surrounded by beatniks and Commies and queers,
and you close the back door, take your shoes off, and follow.

SHE BURNS THE MOTEL
Utah, 1975

I've lived in thrust and throttle,
the kick, the scald, the brand;
my face embraced his bottle,
my mouth has tasted sand.
He only gave me smoulder,
the smoke of hopes grown older,
cigar burns on my shoulder,
and matches in my hand.

I know his grip that bound me,
his breath inside my ear.
The empty road consumes me,
red wind and welts appear.
I leave the bedside crawling;
my instinct says I'm stalling
but, though my God is calling,
I cannot find Him here.

The bills and lawns and houses,
the power mowers and guns,
the boats and Sunday blouses,
grey groups of girls and sons;
there are words the others won't utter,
they gorge on beer and butter
and, while they hide and sputter,
the lost one burns and runs.

Loose in a satin teddy,
ripe on his lips she lies.
Her arms will hold him steady;
her green, unsteady eyes
have seen things that remind her
that life has not refined her.
She'll feel the heat behind her
and rise in stupid surprise.

I'll burn the bitches like money.
They're too far gone to mind,
though her gold hair melts like honey
and the sheet smoke makes them blind
and the timbers crack like dishes.
I'll feel them on my lashes
and bathe in their treacherous ashes,
sweet cells that dance on the wind.

The piss of sparks will mellow.
I will earn what I require
and I'll turn this crap town yellow
and I'll make myself the star.
I was born for the heat to have me;
it's the only thing left that can love me.
Look at my hands above me
and bring me the siren's fire.

THE BLOOD
OF THE JAGERS

And after it rains there's a rainbow
And all of the colors are black
It's not that the colors aren't there
It's just imagination they lack
Everything's the same back in my little town.
SIMON AND GARFUNKEL

Oh daughter, so far, you've only had a taste of icing,
Are you ready now for some cake?
AI

DRAMATIS PERSONAE

Anaïs: a matriarch
Emil: a patriarch
Simon: the son
Ottilie: the daughter
Anu: Simon's wife

PROLOGUE

So Eden sank to grief,
So dawn goes down to day.
Nothing gold can stay.
ROBERT FROST

Anaïs was born on the Isle of Jersey.
She married Emil. Not exactly her type
but getting what she needed would be easy
and twenty-eight was somewhat overripe.

She had two children: Simon ('64)
and Ottilie—unplanned, ten years later.
Simon was a glorious affair;
his sister, she was bookish, ginger. Fatter.

Simon goes off to school and off the rails
but boys, as we all know, can soon be fixed;
they clean up. It's the unloved one who fails.
A golden child can never be eclipsed.

On leaving rehab, Simon's in the Baltics
and meets Anu, a shy mortician's daughter.
You can't engage her on too many topics
but making kids and peace is what we're after.

Emil is good to Ottilie but dies.
Anaïs is left to Simon's care.
Nothing good or loving ever stays:
nothing matters, so we'll leave it there.

LOBBY
Ottilie, 1977

We're making our way through the Four Seasons lobby.
Ma sails through, with the cheek of a bruiser,
and we pass a chrome stroller with a nervous baby
plugged with a rubber Mothercare soother.

She's had a couple of massive Camparis;
she's sick to the marrow with Pa and his droning,
the need to upholster the room with her *sorry*s
for shopping and snapping and sass and complaining.

We're passing the gleam of the oncoming stroller
when she, with a gesture both rash and savant,
plucks out the soother and throws it behind her
(the driver is horrified, wordless, and gaunt),
telling the tot, *Scream as loud as you want.*

HOSE
Anaïs, 1978

The child had it coming,
that jewel you spoiled rotten.
My hair was freshly done,
stacked like a wonderful cake
to match a wonderful dress
to wear to an embassy party.
The little love is four
but malicious to her core
and I swear she came right at me,
the garden hose at full blast.
I only remember the crack
of my hand and the sound of a stone
and the heap of silent poplin
on the ground, the red rivulets running.

THE MARINE ROOM
Ottilie, 1979

Ma takes me out to buy a winter duffle
and, as per tradition, this includes a lunch
at Eaton's swish café. The velvet walls
undulate with reeds of green and gold;
fat amber globes illuminate the booths
crammed with grannies, girls in high stacked shoes,
and men who, lest they might be pegged as old,
festoon themselves in flares and sex-lure smells.
Whenever we go to eat, I get the hunch
that, on this day, perhaps I'm not so awful.

I stir the bowl of mushroom soup. She smiles
a little tightly, pulls the slim Sobranies
from her bag and plucks one out to smoke.
I crinkle out the crackers from their wrap,
smile back, drinking in the scent of her good mood,
the claret suit, the mediocre food.
I've spent hours wishing it wouldn't stop,
hoping I'd be good, the one she'd like,
brighter than the starlets and the grannies,
the chubby starfish plucked out of the shoals.

We are all free. And thus, she must be too,
I think. Look at her smooth, red lips,
the way she clacks her cards on marble counters,
flirts with a manager. Bright and cheery-clear,
she swings the muskrat coat up on her shoulder.

I know I'll be that free when I am older—
as splendid as a Murano chandelier
and engineered for fortunate encounters.
One day, I too will smoke and shop, sink ships,
stand out from mountain vistas others blend into.

FAMILY STANDARDS
Ottilie, 1988

What happened to your Wicked Uncle Guy,
the roué that you used to talk about,
whose topaz cufflinks weighed as much as me?
You say that his piano skills were rough
but village girls leaned in to sigh, to shout
and fiddle with the knot of his cravat.
You told us all the best but not enough.
Nain thought he was a hoot, but weirdly free
with other men, a lizard in his strut,
a never-dying lily in his eye.

Here is the picture where he stands, or stood
back then, a chipper chappy flanked by sheep.
You were in a convent getting tutored
by underwhelming nuns. When you got out,
Nain said, *Guy wedi marw*. Case closed.
Guy was dressed and buried, and downsized
his goings-on by being dead and straight.
Thus fate is kind enough to make things standard
though, in the hills, the lilies curl and weep
and lizards run through fire—as they should.

THE PROPOSITION
Anu, 1994

Kas mii' sōs pal'lu nõvvami'
väiku maa
väiku nurmō?

Is it too much to ask
for a little land
for a little meadow?
"LITANY TO THUNDER," ESTONIAN FOLK SONG

Remembering when we first got together,
nights like when we went to Lake Peipsi
in his Yugo 60, spreading out
the rough wool blanket underneath the stars,
smoking Chesterfields, lust-wriggling tipsy,
gorging on love, the fire, his beaten leather
coat, it got me wondering about
playing again at renegades, *turistid,*

how nice it'd be, now that we've come here,
to ask his mother if she'd take the baby
for a night; we'd slip into town,
catch a band, go and have Chinese
but, when I said it, Simon just went crazy,
spitting into my face that he'd made it clear
my bed was made for him; I'd have to learn
he leaned on me. I couldn't have it easy.

And that was the last suggestion that I made.
So, even though I was only twenty-three,
I followed him to Safeway, Ikea, Lowe's,
set up the basement to look like someone's home,
wheeled the baby to the boiling sea
and back. Spent Friday nights with his mum and dad,
leaned in again, again, to calmly freeze
for pictures. See, he's clean. And happy. Happy.

GRASS
Anu, 1997

When the cop came, I was ready.
I was sitting on the lawn
of some house on 49th,
having changed the baby's diaper
right in front of the big front window
in between the toys and sprinklers.

It's been seven months already,
seven months of my life gone.
Day on week on month on month—
stay-at-home looks good on paper
but that's what made my mother hollow;
that's what turned us into drinkers.

Will my baby's love be heady
like how Simon loves his mum—
sugary blarney filling his mouth—
when I get a different flavour
(palm and sweat and soggy pillow)
every time he fails or angers?

Come and get the little lady,
Constable. The car has room
for all of us. For all our wrath.
Me on the lawn of the lucky neighbour,
hands in the grass in twilight's shadow,
rubbing in shit with all ten fingers

THE MISTAKE
Ottilie, 2003

Ma swore there was a barbecue that evening.
They told her that there wasn't, and she went blank,
crumpled like a teary, trampled flower.
She realized that she was far from well
but also that the night would linger empty—
no magic hour, no drinks, no summer love.

When we were little, Ma lived by a love
of fancy, in a sundress cut for evening,
draining the jeroboam till it was empty,
shooting the flirting look (a furtive blank).
The garden party swing, she did it well.
(See her bouffanted, smiling, in full flower!)

Once married, a woman is a rare, plucked flower
set in glass for someone else to love,
a wishing penny dropped in a country well
by curious walkers on a humid evening.
She sells herself as a screen, seductively blank,
a curving flask of promise, full and empty

but, rather than submit herself to empty
man-gruff conversations, Ma would flower,
charm the world to death, outshine the blank
dollies in their Pucci. How they'd love
to find her now and throttle her one evening,
ripe with rage at what she did too well.

But Simon hasn't ended up too well:
He hates his job. His bank account is empty.
He settles in for football every evening.
Anu has never seen a card, a flower,
but wears a purple smudge (a sign of love;
when asked, she smiles in vagueness, draws a blank).

But my son's life, Ma thinks, *is just a blank*
cheque waiting to be filled. It could go well.
His plaintive pleading must be due to love—
when he tells her that the giant fridge is empty
and a man needs cable to go with his milk and flour
or that he has *a plan,* evening after evening.

No plans, my love, says Pa. The calendar's blank.
And the summer evening rolls out—a yawning well
drained empty by her bloom and her own black flower.

THE BARBARIAN INVASION
2016

Cultivated as Catholic from her cradle,
trained by nuns, a fount of guilt:
who knew genetics made her able,
forged to the teeth as a fuck-you Celt?

When Simon came at her that night,
rabid with rage and impure cocaine,
she brained him, hobbling out in flight
to the neighbour's door in the pouring rain.

She came with the broken cane and her knitting
to the cops and the medics in dismal dawn,
her Pius XI consciousness never admitting
she'd handed her boy to the hounds of Arawn.

NEIGHBOURHOOD WATCH

2017

We saw that woman (is she German? Finnish?)
walking with your mum, who stopped to chat
with a neighbour but was hastily pulled along.
We wondered, then, if something might be wrong;
her arms were limp and her jacket was frayed and wet
but, really, it seemed safer just to vanish.

We knew that, every week, she went to church
with Tom from up the street but suddenly stopped,
and that visitors had dribbled to a drip.
It should have stood out like a swollen lip
and maybe we suspected something slipped
but none of us were rude enough to search.

You know, we always knew it in the end,
that something was amiss. Your mother's sweet;
please tell her when you see her there, wherever.
Marge and I know, when the whole shebang blows over,
she'll thank us all for being so discreet,
watching it all from the window, like a friend.

BEST PRACTICE
Ottilie, 2018

Your emotions make you a monster.
DEAD KENNEDYS

We thought it would be over soon enough.
He'd listen to the facts and move along,
find a job, a house, someone to love,
but we were wrong.

The guys we knew from way back when went clean;
our much sought-after punk lords of misrule
took up cycling, ran a snow machine,
went back to school

while weary girlfriends (Bev or Jane or Bree)
coaxed them into getting on the ladder:
finding a Special out by the PNE
they'd fix together.

If kids appeared, they'd step up to the plate,
cart them up to soccer on the Drive,
put on an act they had a cleaner slate,
master the high-five.

You'd see them hauling speakers at a gig,
drinking Cokes and fondly reminiscing
about that night (the ketamine! the wig!)
a friend went missing.

We told ourselves that maybe they were sellouts
but, though they thickened up, becoming squares,
a part of us inside was somewhat jealous.
The God that spares

did not spare him. He wouldn't ever soften
but curled his evils into my life and yours
and that is why our mother says so often
Check the doors.

EPILOGUE: HER MUSTANG

He promised she would have a stuccoed house,
a flag, a fountain, a flight of blood-wood stairs,
a tree for cherries, another for Anjou pears,
winters down in Aspen, just because.
There was a pond of bulging copper koi,
a spray of rhododendron at the gate,
a gardener she swore was worth his weight
in glads; the au pairs (too refined to stay).
But, in the halls, the light suspended motes
like locusts pausing to destroy the field,
the sprinkler chattered horrors in the dusk
as sparrows tore at one another's throats.
Her children wouldn't wash or nap or yield;
she knew them all too well to even ask.

She oversaw the tray of morning tea,
stood, bleached with sun, to watch his car pull out,
received the caterers, gave serious thought
to osso bucco, Cherries Jubilee,
swept dust from the Varley's gilded frame,
drank Metrecal with Seagram's. Fell asleep,
grew older every time Emil would quip
about the way the dinners stayed the same
or why she had to nap or drink or cry
as the maples shed their sludge and the wet snow fell
and the purple sky sat heavily and stared
at no one. And twenty more years went by.
The children grew and left, as children will,
and television taught her to be scared.

And now she sits in the plush and airy suite,
gasping onto the skyline of the young,
vaguely alarmed to find herself among
the old. I never knew her to be sweet
but, poking my strudel, ask her how she slept,
how she likes her crafting or *The Crown*.
I haven't touched on how I let her down
or where we were when the hope inside her snapped,
when the men laughed warmly when she got things wrong
or snickered when she sashayed through a room,
when the golden child grew up and robbed her blind.
I want her to pack and leave, climb into her Mustang
one morning in '75 (clogs, perfume),
drive off, and leave the mess we are behind.

CLEVER LITTLE DRAGON: ON *HETTY DORVAL*

PROLOGUE: THE GENIUS OF MY HOME
Frankie

I am so glad I am what I have become—
sensible and true to my upbringing.
It all comes back: the genius of my home,
those gloves upon the floor, and Hetty singing
softly now in French, standing diverted,
her face so soft, so calm. She understands
what it means to have life complicated
(callers with their trilbies in their hands,
a cake, some fruit, a stash of helpful prayers;
their cluttering concerns are so unwanted).
What is Hetty when she never cares,
sensuous, unsorry, never haunted?
I cast her out (her furs, her vague affairs)
and watch her back descend the narrow stairs.

THE GEESE
Frankie

We meet along the road as she descends,
sitting on her glossy little mare,
and move along in silence, almost friends.
Against the aura of her yellow hair,
her cheekbones arch towards the perfect ears,
the nose (a flirt's) tilts upwards. When she turns,
her face is tender to the point of tears,
her voice so light its timbre almost burns.
I'm formless, undiscovered, lacking words
until the arrow slides across the sky
above the sage and shale. The augur birds,
the geese of Lytton. With a startled cry
Hetty asks, *Will it ever come again?*
But, bridle-wise, I cannot tell her when.

THE CLAIM
Frankie

What they don't know (or do) is that they're *ours*.
My parents staked a claim on them. It's done.
Their gormless boys assist us with the chores:
fixing fences, shielding shoots from sun.
Or maybe not. Maybe they're never there,
those *Indians* of ours. They can't commit;
they vanish on a wagonload somewhere,
then reappear at the Depot, faces set
in curious/incurious disdain.
The younger children, chorus-like but quiet,
watch us as we approach a woman (in vain)
or follow another wreathed in the scent of riot.
Thanks to our Joe Charley and Charley Joe,
the game is up. Soon, everyone will know.

A WORD OF PRAYER
Frankie

Mr Thompson, minister, pays a call
and Hetty hides me. From behind the door
I watch her (seen) and him (unseen). For all
his questioning, the dividends are poor.
Is your husband English? Answer: no.
Is he coming soon? She blocks the blade.
I see you read. My wife's the same, you know.
She'd love to call. She stops him, unafraid.
Though churchless, she accepts a word of prayer,
clasps her hands and plays along, unkneeling.
Hiding, I watch the saint suspended there;
she thanks him, as she clasps his hands with feeling,
launching him down the hill with a quaint goodbye
(and yet, and yet I love her till I die).

PEEPING TOM

They say that Hester's *husband* is in town
so Frankie steals along with Ernestine.
The window frames the woman in her gown,
curled on a sofa. What can that smile mean?
Is she happy when the tweed back rises,
moves to the fire, a square hand packing his pipe?
Is she the only? Is she but one of his prizes?
Does he love her? (Is she even his type?)
Nobody knows. For now she's bent on giving,
tilting her face in the glow of the lamp and the flame.
She takes him in and lets him play at wiving
and the girl at the window, ashamed she ever came,
shuffles in the frost and the dying roots,
watching the unnamed man in tall black boots.

A WOMAN OF NO REPUTATION
Frankie

They know it's time to set the record straight.
I want them to. I feel left outside.
That woman, Father says, is second-rate
to say the least. Even if I denied
all evildoing, said we only sang
in French, drank tea, and worshipped wild geese,
it wouldn't change a thing. I've found my gang,
the only unit that can bring me peace.
These are the eyes you need, the family says,
this is the future. Mother inside Father,
Father inside Empire; follow what he does,
do as they do, aloof, entwined, together.
You need us like the timid rose needs water.
Come to my arms, my funny little daughter.

THE FREAK SHOW
Frankie

Hustle past the hot dogs and the swings,
the Ferris wheel, the dunk tank, and the carnies
who watch the children pop balloons, toss rings
in uniformed, uninterested armies.
Come and see the Lobster Boy! His hands
have blistered into claws. Perhaps they're real,
perhaps they're not. You'll have to ask his fans.
If you asked him, he'd probably say *big deal,*
I'm different from you. Like other freaks
I generate speculation, hearty shudders.
I can keep you gossiping for weeks
for I am ruined, worse than all the others.
But I know something that'll really throw you.
Follow me to Hetty's, and I'll show you.

SLEEPING BEAUTY
Frankie

At Mrs Richards's school, in our top-floor room,
one window faces out to English Bay
while the other side looks over Lost Lagoon
and to the mountains, large, primordial, and grey.
The mirror on the wall has a cheapish frame
but perfect glass. Cradle-like it holds
the image of the Sleeping Beauty, tame
as a dozing cat. The languid granite folds,
scattered with late spring snow and lilac dusk,
are ours, suspended for our own keeping.
The proper schoolgirl knows who she can trust
and why we leave the living beauty sleeping.
I've learned that rocks and rivers equal damage;
reflection is much easier to manage.

GIVE IT TO ME, FRANK

Ellen Burnaby belongs to Frank;
being at one with him, she knows the score,
what women do, what the neighbours will think,
how to save the child you adore.
Here is the house—The Menace's old dwelling,
scrubbed of its vices, quaint as a porcelain bowl.
Let's take it over, she says. I know they're selling.
Open the window to empty the room of her soul.
Consider, then, all Menace-memory finished,
pleasures cuckoo-tipped into the river
while they settle in her place, no charms diminished
but sanctified. The keys are theirs forever.
This is the start of goodbye. The adult's tomorrow,
and the passing train snakes by and wails in sorrow.

YOU CAN TAKE IT FROM ME / THE SHIP

Hetty tracks the women to the rail,
cornering them in the cold and saline dark.
You were my friend once. For a little while.
She knows she lives with the other Hester's mark,
the other Hester's history. She pleads
to be unspoken of, for they are kind;
she's moving to the comfort that she needs,
leaving the sheen of loucheness all behind.
Can they both say nothing? Can she marry,
slip into respectable? The mother
hearkens to the tremble, feels sorry,
vows (with the girl) to show her clearer weather
although the urge to be informed is clinging,
and somewhere, in the distance, a phone is ringing.

REPUTATION, MISTRESS, SHANGHAI

Passing the crumpets, Mrs K-C dishes the dirt.
Scene: Shanghai. A Frenchman and his lady
(the latter: a school friend with a tender heart)
settle down, prepare to have a baby,
when in comes the stranger. She drives the husband mad,
plucks him like a fruit, that riding teacher,
unstables him; it ends in suicide.
And the stranger leaves. You see, it's in her nature:
Frenchman to oilman, oilman on to lord—
who will care? We hold her in our hands.
We've named her, and we have the final word,
and we all know how the tale of Hetty ends.
She's lighter than a leaf. She doesn't *mind*.
Who gives a damn if history's unkind?

TERRA INCOGNITA
Frankie

O, my cousins, let me introduce you
(handsome Dick, young, elongating Molly)
to Hetty—now Lady Connott. She'll seduce you
but getting any closer would be folly.
See how sad she looks, in her widow's weeds,
her ermine stole. To the young, she's very charming.
She'll hold you until she's taken what she needs;
consider this a blood relation's warning.
Yes. Let her have your number. Let her visit,
let her charm the birds in St James Square,
let her make her loneliness explicit.
Know it's vapour. Know it isn't there.
I'll hand her over. Just know I've staked a claim:
I own her reputation and her name.

ANY REAL LOVE
Mrs Broom

I am the mouse who hides behind the scenes,
the overseeing ghost, woman of doors,
breaking my back in the usual routines—
ordering jam and flowers from the stores,
or getting your damn piano at the station.
At home, I'm the companion by the fire,
bumped down to servant (not without frustration)
if ever intruders come. If it sounds dire,
it is. You'll never know the need to need,
you'll never shroud yourself with crumpled grief
or anger. You're so selfish, hard to read.
You're blithe. You're ruin. You're a little thief.
You've done all right by me but failed me, Hester;
your artlessness will lead to your disaster.

EPILOGUE: VIENNA

The Gonzagagasse flat, home of the Sterns,
is dim and stunned. Outside, a sky of lead
squashes the ancient spires. A visitor discerns
the escritoire, the Biedermeier bed,
the baby grand with Szymanowska scattered,
the Meissen demitasse on Jules's side table,
cracked. If love and Lytton really mattered,
if friendship plodded on as it was able,
maybe this wouldn't have happened. The neighbour woman
pointing her finger *(Juden! Juden!)*, the door
kicked in, the muffled sound of human
consternation. Frau Stern meanders into her war,
light to a fault, diffused, unknown, misread
as flocks of fleeing geese scream overhead.

NOTES

"Pierogis": *Manti* are dumplings popular in Central Asia, as well as in the South Caucasus, Iran, Afghanistan, Pakistan, Russia, and other post-Soviet nations. Boiled or steamed, they usually consist of a dough wrapper stuffed with spiced meat.

"Bryce McMillan, 38, Futures Trader, Stuck at the Men's Retreat" was inspired by Dylan Thomas's "Refusal to Mourn the Death, by Fire, of a Child in London."

"The Lipstick Effect" makes reference to the following lipstick shades: Fire Down Below and Dolce Vita (NARS), Pirate and Vamp (Chanel), Lustering (MAC), and Cherries in the Snow (Revlon).

"Family Standards": *Nain* (Welsh): Grandmother. *Guy wedi marw:* Guy is dead.

"The Barbarian Invasion": Pope Pius XI was head of the Catholic Church from 1922 until his death in 1939. Arawn is the warlike Celtic god of the dead, revenge, and terror, and features prominently in Welsh mythology.

Clever Little Dragon: On Hetty Dorval: Ethel Wilson's 1947 short novel *Hetty Dorval* is a much-misunderstood (and underrated) Canadian work about a young girl living in the BC Interior who encounters, becomes infatuated with, and then betrays a mysterious divorcee who is herself the product of a scandalous affair. Long portrayed as a morality tale focusing on the "Innocence vs. Experience" theme, Wilson's book is a sly take on how prejudice, moral stagnation, and class mobility combine to misrepresent vulnerability and strength and target feminine figures who dare to survive and take delight from the world on their own terms. The protagonist, Frankie, encounters Hetty while she is out riding in the hills around Lytton, and the two form a tenuous friendship. Frankie's parents are pricked to action regarding a number of rumours that swirl around Hetty: that she is a home wrecker, a gold digger, and an adventuress. Frankie is sent off, first to boarding school in Vancouver and then to England, to stay with genteel relations. As the novel progresses, Frankie is subtly corroded by the effects of her colonialist and class-sensitive upbringing. Her untainted empathy with the childlike Hetty gives way to the effects of an inherited value system; she rejects Hetty as a young adult, casting her forth to the uncertain waters of World War II. Hetty, who we hear has remarried (for the third time) to a Jewish businessman, is most likely doomed to be swallowed up by the forces of history and the appetites of intolerance. To my mind, *Hetty Dorval* is the great unsung Canadian horror novel.

ACKNOWLEDGEMENTS

"Seventeen" (previously "One Love"), "The Lipstick
Effect," and "Best Practice" all appeared, in some version
or another, in the pages of the *Walrus*. "Hollywood. North."
appeared online in *Dusie*. Thanks are due to the editors.
"Triptych: American Wives" (formerly "The Home
Song") and "Epilogue: Her Mustang" were featured as a
joint creative component as part of my Comprehensive
Examination Papers towards my PHD at McMaster
University. "*Clever Little Dragon*: On *Hetty Dorval*" was
conceived as a creative submission for the graduate course
ENGL 783: Novels of the Margins. I send my thanks and
respect to Dr Jeffery Donaldson, Dr Melinda Gough, and
Dr Roger Hyman, mentors and comrades-in-arms all.

I would like to thank Jason Guriel, for taking the time
(and the red pen/blowtorch) to see to these poems. I
count myself as very lucky to have had his expert eye
and ear at my disposal. Thanks also to John Sweet for
plucking out the irregularities, and to Stephen Duffy,

who was kind enough to contribute the image for the cover. Finally, gratitude is due to Daniel Wells and the team at Biblioasis for standing behind me and this book.

As ever the big love goes out to Dragan (who has elevated the phrase *What now?* to new sentimental heights) and Gavra, my indefatigable tech support.

Alexandra Oliver was born in Vancouver, BC. She
is the author of *Meeting the Tormentors in Safeway*
(Biblioasis 2013), which received the 2014 Pat Lowther
Award, and *Let the Empire Down* (Biblioasis 2016)
which was shortlisted for the same. A graduate of
the Stonecoast MFA in Creative Writing Program at
the University of Southern Maine, she is currently
completing a PHD in English and Cultural Studies at
McMaster University in Hamilton, Ontario.

Printed by Imprimerie Gauvin
Gatineau, Québec